The first year of a baby's life is precious and life-affirming . . . if you manage to remember them through the sleep deprivation, anxiety, and hours of advice everyone you've ever met wants to give you. Thankfully, *Hooray New Baby!* is here to help you record the true story of your baby's important first year so memories are never fuzzy!

This baby book, written and designed by illustrator Veronica Dearly, is filled with prompts and exercises to encourage you to write the story of your new baby.

How few hours of sleep did you get the first week after your baby came home? Was your baby's first Holiday a sugar-high-filled delight, or a toppled-over-tree and broken ornament nightmare? This baby book goes from being an exercise in maintaining your sanity to a sentimental keepsake of frank, sweet observations about that special first year of your baby's life as you fill its pages.

As functional as it is hilarious, *Hooray New Baby!* is a wonderful way to remember year one of parenthood so you don't lose the memories—along with your mind.

Carefully remove this page so you can personalize this charming book with wonderful facts about your new little one!

Use quality scrapbook adhesives for attaching photos and any keepsakes. Always allow ink and glue to dry before closing or turning pages.

Brimming with creative inspiration, how-to projects, and useful information to enrich your everyday life, Quarto Knows is a favorite destination for those pursuing their interests and passions. Visit our site and dig deeper with our books into your area of interest: Quarto Creates, Quarto Cooks, Quarto Homes, Quarto Lives, Quarto Drives, Quarto Explores, Quarto Gifts, or Quarto Kids.

© 2018 by Veronica Dearly

First published in 2018 by Rock Point,
an imprint of The Quarto Group,
142 West 36th Street, 4th Floor
New York, NY 10018 USA
T (212) 779-4972 **F** (212) 779-6058
www.QuartoKnows.com

Rock Point titles are also available at discount for retail, wholesale, promotional, and bulk purchase. For details, contact the Special Sales Manager by email at specialsales@quarto.com or by mail at The Quarto Group, Attn: Special Sales Manager, 401 Second Avenue North, Suite 310, Minneapolis, MN 55401, USA.

10 9 8 7 6 5 4 3 2 1

ISBN: 1-978-1-63106-491-3

Editorial Director: Rage Kindelsperger
Managing Editor: Erin Canning
Project Editor: Keyla Hernández
Cover and Interior Design: Veronica Dearly
Design Manager: Philip Buchanan

Printed in China

Hooray NEW BABY!

A KEEPSAKE BOOK FOR OUR precious, real-life BABY

BY VERONICA DEARLY

ROCK POINT

Before YOU WERE BORN

I KNOW YOU WON'T BELIEVE
THIS, BUT WE WERE AROUND
before YOU WERE BORN.

Mommy WAS A ....
AND Daddy WAS A.................
WE LIVED IN ....
AND WE THOUGHT HAVING A BABY
WOULD BE...........................

Mommy & Daddy

BEFORE PREGNANCY

US BEFORE YOU

Mommy WAS MOST EXCITED
ABOUT ....
....
AND MOST SCARED ABOUT
....
....
OVERALL SHE FELT...................
....

Daddy WAS MOST EXCITED
ABOUT ....
....
AND MOST SCARED ABOUT
....
....
OVERALL HE FELT...................
....

Best (+ FUNNIEST) Reactions TO THE NEWS THAT You Were Coming

When we told ....

HE/SHE/THEY SAID ....

this made us feel ....

When we told ....

HE/SHE/THEY SAID ....

this made us feel ....

When we told ....

HE/SHE/THEY SAID ....

this made us feel ....

Scan Photo

(Scan Photo)

HERE YOU WERE AT ..... WEEKS.

THE INTERNET TOLD ME THAT YOU WERE THE SIZE OF A .... WHICH WAS USEFUL.

WE THOUGHT YOU LOOKED LIKE A .... SO WE WERE GRATEFUL THAT YOU TURNED OUT TO BE A BABY.

Mommy HAD AN........................ PREGNANCY WITH YOU, SHE CRAVED........................ AND MOANED MOST ABOUT.............. ....

We FIRST FELT YOU MOVE AT .... WEEKS

You WERE DUE ON....................

Bump photo

(Bump Photo)

On the Day You Were Born

THE DATE WAS ....

AND IT WAS .... OUTSIDE.

♫ ....
....
by ....
was no. 1 on
the MUSIC
CHARTS.

THE
....
....
....
....
was the front page
of the NEWSPAPER

a gallon of
milk cost
....
and a pint
of beer cost
....
(WE BOUGHT
.... MORE OFTEN)

....
....
was running
the country

hipsters were
drinking
....
and wearing
....

and the average
house price was
....

Place YOU WERE BORN ....

IF YOU WEREN'T BEING BORN ON THAT DAY, Mommy & Daddy

WOULD HAVE BEEN ....

You WERE BORN at ...., you WERE .... long,

AND WEIGHED .... WITH .... hair

AND .... eyes. We looked at you and felt

....

You looked like ....

....

WE DIDN'T REALIZE HOW

....

IT WOULD BE.

You were ....

The first
photo of
Baby

The first Photo of You

(Your FIRST Moments)

THE STORY OF THE FIRST FEW HOURS OF YOUR LIFE:

....

....

....

....

....

....

....

On Your First Day

You wore..

YOU SLEPT FOR ..... HOURS. YOU WERE VISITED BY

....

We had to change your diaper .... times.

YOU LIKED BEING ....

and cried when ....

Messages FROM YOUR Visitors

FROM.........................

FROM.........................

FROM.........................

FROM.........................

Well-meaning YET Terrible UNSOLICITED ADVICE PEOPLE 🙂 GAVE US ABOUT YOU.....

. . . . TOLD US	. . . . THOUGHT THAT	. . . . SAID
. . . . SAID	. . . . TOLD US	. . . . THOUGHT THAT
. . . . THOUGHT THAT	. . . . SAID	. . . . TOLD US

OUR HOPES + WISHES FOR YOU

We hope you are...

and you know...

and that you grow to be...

We hope you're not....

and that you never...

and always feel...

We hope you're not afraid of...

and that you always remember...

3 Wishes for you

Your FIRST Worldly POSSESSIONS

FIRST TOY

was a............

....

from................

....

FIRST BLANKET

was................

from................

SO SNUGGLY + ...

FIRST WHEELS

we first pushed you

around in a ....

....

....

....

FIRST BOOK

your first

book was................

.... IT WAS

ABOUT................

Things WE WERE TOLD About Babies

(AND WHETHER THEY TURNED OUT TO BE TRUE OR NOT)

....
....

Comments

TRUTH	/10

....

....

TRUTH /10

Comments

....
....
....

Comments

....

....

TRUTH	/10

Comments

TRUTH /10

....

....

Comments

....

....

....

....

....

....

Where we lived

Our Home

WE LIVED AT..................................
....
....

WHEN WE FIRST BROUGHT
YOU HOME. YOU WERE.......
DAYS OLD AND WE FELT

....

EVEN THOUGH YOU WERE A
TINY BABY AND COULDN'T HAVE
CARED LESS ABOUT DECÓR, WE
WENT WITH A ....
THEME WITH.............................
WALLS.

Baby's Room

Baby's Room

(Our "FIRSTS")

YOU

1st time YOU THREW UP DOWN SOMEBODY'S BACK

....

1st time YOU GOT UP EVERY SINGLE HOUR IN THE NIGHT

....

1st time YOU LET US EAT A HOT MEAL TOGETHER

....

1st time FILL IN YOUR OWN!

....

US

1st time WE LOOKED AT EACH OTHER AND REALIZED WE WERE WAY OUT OF OUR DEPTH

....

1st time WE FORGOT TO TAKE A CHANGE OF CLOTHES FOR YOU OUT SOMEWHERE AND IT BACKFIRED CATASTROPHICALLY

....

1st time ONE OF US FELL ASLEEP IN AN UNUSUAL PLACE DUE TO BABY INDUCED TIREDNESS

....

1st time FILL IN YOUR OWN!

....

Our "FIRSTS"

YOU

1st time

....

1st time

....

1st time

....

1st time

....

US

1st time

....

1st time

....

1st time

....

1st time

....

Behind Your Name

WE DECIDED THAT YOUR **NAME** WOULD BE:

BECAUSE...

apparently, IT MEANS ....

We also liked ...., ..., and.................

IF **Mommy** HAD HER WAY, YOU'D BE CALLED
....

IF **Daddy** HAD HIS WAY, YOU'D BE CALLED
....

Thank Goodness for Compromise!

YOUR MIDDLE NAME MEANS..

....

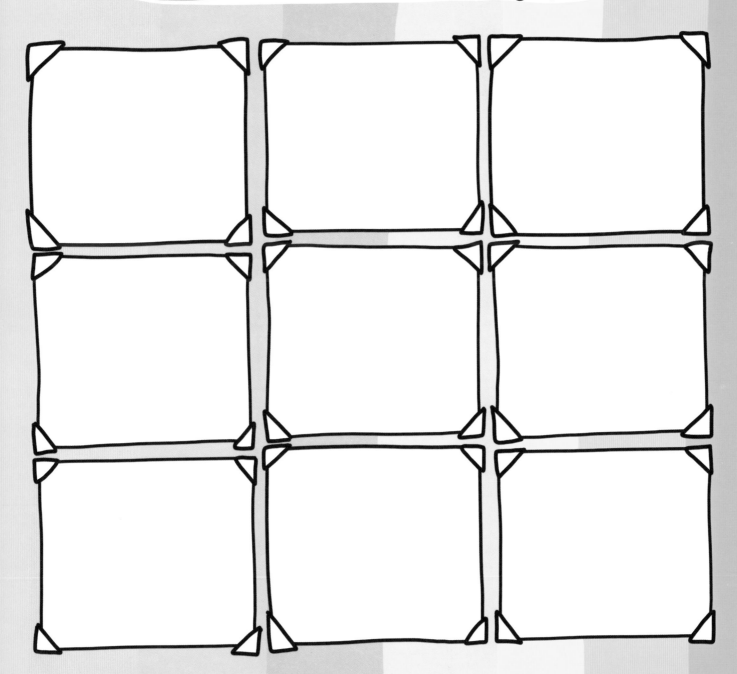

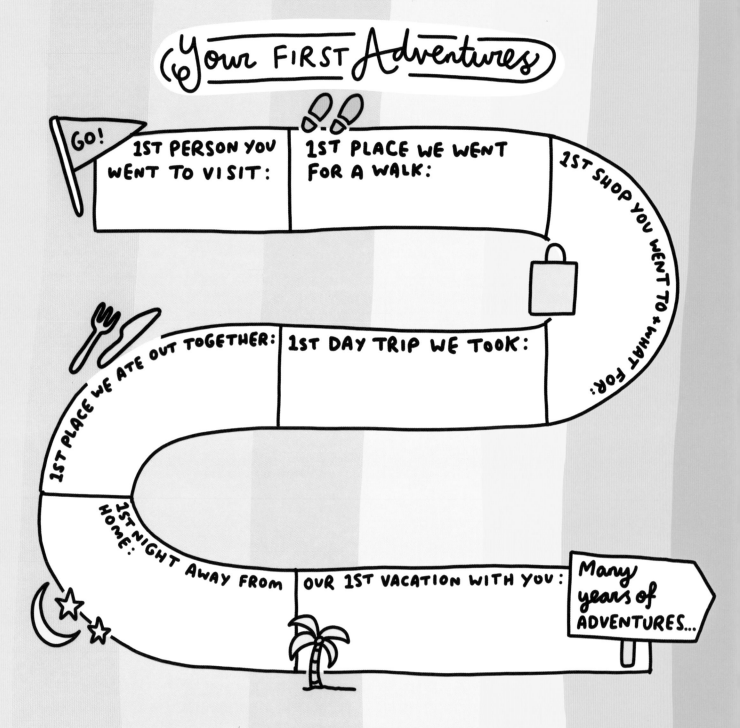

Weird Stuff YOU DID

BABIES CAN BE *weird* SOMETIMES, AND YOU WERE NO EXCEPTION.
TO PROVE THIS, HERE IS AN EXHAUSTIVE CATALOG OF WEIRDNESS:

Date	Weird Thing You Did...	Weird Scale out of 10

A Day in the Life

A TYPICAL DAY WHEN YOU WERE TINY + NEW

. . . .

. . . .

. . . .

. . . .

. . . .

. . . .

. . . .

. . . .

. . . .

THINGS YOU DO

- ☐ . . . .
- ☐ . . . .
- ☐ . . . .
- ☐ . . . .

STATS

YOU WAKE UP FOR THE DAY AT

. . . .

YOU HAVE . . . . . . NAPS EVERY DAY.

YOU MOSTLY EAT . . . .

. . . .

YOUR FAVORITE THING TO DO IS

. . . .

A Day in the Life

A TYPICAL DAY WHEN YOU WERE 3 MONTHS OLD

....

....

....

....

....

....

....

....

THINGS YOU DO

☐ ....

☐ ....

☐ ....

☐ ....

STATS

YOU WAKE UP FOR THE DAY AT

....

YOU HAVE......NAPS EVERY DAY.

YOU MOSTLY EAT...................

....

YOUR FAVORITE THING TO DO IS

....

A Day IN THE Life

A TYPICAL DAY WHEN YOU WERE 6 MONTHS OLD

....

....

....

....

....

....

....

....

THINGS YOU DO

☐ ....

☐ ....

☐ ....

☐ ....

STATS

YOU WAKE UP FOR THE DAY AT

....

YOU HAVE ...... NAPS EVERY DAY.

YOU MOSTLY EAT ....

....

YOUR FAVORITE THING TO DO IS

....

A Day in the Life

A TYPICAL DAY WHEN YOU WERE A YEAR OLD

....

....

....

....

....

....

....

....

....

THINGS YOU DO

- [ ] ....
- [ ] ....
- [ ] ....
- [ ] ....

STATS

YOU WAKE UP FOR THE DAY AT

....

YOU HAVE......NAPS EVERY DAY.

YOU MOSTLY EAT.....................

....

YOUR FAVORITE THING TO DO IS

....

COMPULSORY TRADITIONAL BABY *Milestones*

SMILE

GIGGLE

HOLDING HEAD UP

ROLLING OVER

SITTING UP

FIRST WORD (HI)

CRAWLING

STANDING UP

FIRST TOOTH

TRIED SOLID FOOD

FIRST STEPS

SLEPT ALL NIGHT

YOUR FIRST _holiday Season_

THE FIRST HOLIDAY WE CELEBRATED WITH YOU WAS

....

YOU WERE ...... MONTHS OLD AND WE CELEBRATED BY

....

....

AND SPENT IT WITH

....

....

YOUR FAVORITE PART WAS

....

....

....

_Us_
- _Celebrating_ -

On The Big Day

YOUR FAVORITE *holiday Season*

YOUR FAVORITE HOLIDAY WAS

....

YOU WERE ...... MONTHS OLD AND WE CELEBRATED BY

....

....

AND SPENT IT WITH

....

....

YOUR FAVORITE PART WAS

....

....

....

Us Celebrating

On The Big Day

(Your FAVORITE Things)

 PLACE...

 TOY...

COLOR...

SONG... ♪♫

BOOK...

🍴 FOOD...

CHARACTER...

HI WORD...

GAME...

LOOK at your TINY LITTLE baby toes!

GRAB SOME BABY-FRIENDLY INK OR PAINT

AND GET STAMPING!

WHEN YOU WERE JUST ..... DAYS OLD

'LOOK' at how your LITTLE FEET grew!)

GRAB SOME BABY-FRIENDLY INK OR PAINT

AND GET STAMPING!

WHEN YOU WERE A WHOLE year OLD

(One Whole YEAR IN)

<u>Somehow</u> A YEAR HAS GONE BY! AND *what a year it was!*

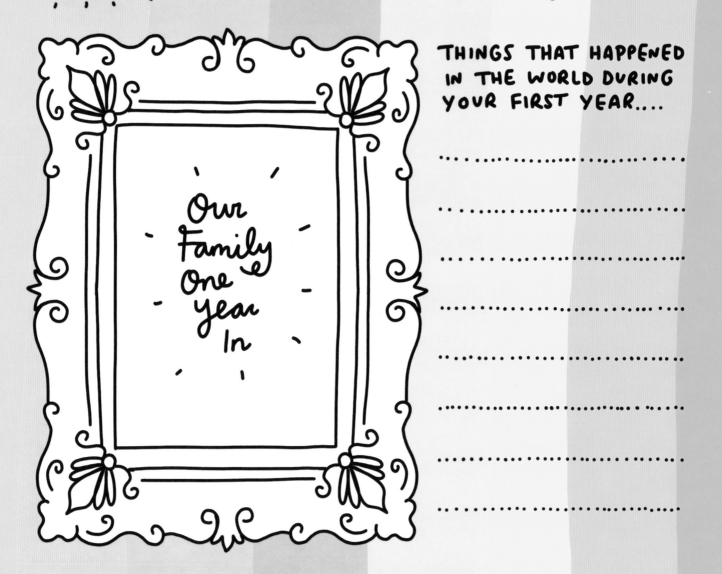

Our Family One Year In

THINGS THAT HAPPENED
IN THE WORLD DURING
YOUR FIRST YEAR....

....

....

....

....

....

....

....

(Your FIRST Birthday)

On the Big Day

you on your Birthday

WHAT WE DID TO celebrate:

....

....

....

....

LOVELY gifts YOU RECEIVED:

....

....

....

....

Party Time

How We Celebrated

HOW YOU'VE Changed

Tiny Baby Photo

This little person...

12-Month-Old Baby Photo

...grew into this!

WEIGHT:

HEIGHT:

PERSONALITY:

WEIGHT:

HEIGHT:

PERSONALITY:

What a difference a year makes!

KEEPSAKES FOR OUR
precious, real-life BABY

Gifts YOU WERE GIVEN just FOR being born